Pre-Raphaelite
paintings and drawings

Arthur Hughes

Illustration for Christina
Rossetti's, *Sing-Song*

Ashmolean · Christie's handbooks

Pre-Raphaelite
paintings and drawings

Jon Whiteley

Sponsored by
Christie's Fine Art Auctioneers
London

Phaidon · Christie's Limited
in association
with the Ashmolean Museum

First published 1989
Phaidon · Christie's Limited
Musterlin House, Jordan Hill Road, Oxford OX2 8DP

Published in association with the Ashmolean Museum
Text and illustrations © The University of Oxford:
Ashmolean Museum, Oxford 1989
Published in paperback by the Ashmolean Museum, 1989

ISBN   0 7148 8068 X (hardback)
       0 907849 94 6 (paperback)

Cover illustration: *Proserpine* by Dante Gabriel Rossetti

Designed by Cole design unit, Reading
Set in Versailles by Meridian Phototypesetting Limited
Printed and bound in Great Britain by
Roundwood Press, Kineton, Warwickshire

Introduction

The Pre-Raphaelite Brotherhood was formed in London in September 1848 by five painters, William Holman Hunt, Dante Gabriel Rossetti, John Everett Millais, James Collinson and Frederick Stephens, together with a sculptor, Thomas Woolner and a writer, William Michael Rossetti, Dante's brother. Although the painters outnumbered the others, the idea of Pre-Raphaelite sculpture was taken seriously in the early years and poetry, always important, became increasingly influential in Rossetti's circle. It is difficult to think of another group of artists that wrote so much poetry or painted so many pictures inspired by it. The 'List of Immortals', those who 'revealed vast visions of beauty to mankind', which Hunt and Rossetti compiled in 1848, includes surprisingly few painters before Raphael. Christ, with five stars, heads the list; the remainder is dominated by poets. Shakespeare and the author of Job alone occupy the second division; Leonardo da Vinci is the only painter in the third division which otherwise includes Dante, Chaucer, Keats, Shelley, Landor, Thackeray and Homer; apart from Fra Angelico (included, no doubt, more for his blameless life than for his art) and Raphael, both of whom appear in the fourth division, painters appear prominently only in the lowest class and even here, the choice, which includes Hogarth, Giorgione, Titian, Tintoretto, Poussin, Michelangelo and Wilkie, is hardly 'Pre-Raphaelite' in any obvious sense. The list shows that Rossetti, in particular, had a passionate taste for romantic and medieval literature, that Hunt had read Ruskin's praise of the Venetians in *Modern Painters* and that neither knew very much at all about Italian art before the age of

Raphael. 'They intend' said John Ruskin, in a letter to *The Times* in 1851 'to return to early days in this one point only – that, so far as in them lies, they will draw either what they see, or what they suppose might have been the actual facts of the scene they desire to represent, irrespective of any conventional rules of picture-making and they have chosen their unfortunate tho' not inaccurate name because all artists did this before Raphael's time, and after Raphael's time did not this but thought to paint fair pictures rather than represent stern facts'.

This is very curious as a description of art before Raphael. Even as an account of the Pre-Raphaelites, it is only partly true, describing Hunt's painstaking imitation of the natural world, but making no allowance for Rossetti's stylish evocation of the Middle Ages which combined uneasily with the Pre-Raphaelite ideal of 'stern facts' and became, in time, an alternative to it.

Rossetti entered the Royal Academy School in 1844 but was bored by the curriculum which left little space for the imagination. He turned for help in 1848 to Ford Madox Brown, a painter who was about eight years older than Rossetti and his friends and who, unlike them, had seen early Italian art in Italy at first hand. More importantly, during his stay in Rome, Brown had been influenced by the Pre-Raphaelite taste of the Nazarenes, a group of German artists in Rome who had, like the Brotherhood, reacted against their academic training and had turned to the early Italians for an alternative to the dark paint and conventional gestures and expressions of the art school. It is not surprising that Rossetti, whose father was a Dante scholar and Professor of Italian literature at King's College, found the early Italian manner of Brown's work so attractive. Rossetti identified, obsessively, with his namesake, Dante Alighieri, the thirteenth century poet whose introspective, autobiographical romance, the *Vita Nuova* (New Life), inspired many of his pictures.

Poetry also brought Rossetti and Hunt together for the first time. Hunt sent a picture inspired by an episode from the *Eve of St. Agnes* to the Royal Academy exhibition in 1848 which attracted Rossetti who also admired the poetry of Keats. He introduced himself to Hunt who, in turn, introduced himself to his protégé, the talented and likeable John Everett Millais. Unlike Hunt or Rossetti, Millais did not have the temperament to be a great original, but he was a ready convert.

For a time, the Brotherhood followed a common purpose. Their drawings acquired a spiky similarity which is present but less evident in their finished works. They adopted a manner of painting on a wet, white ground, based on the ancient technique of fresco painting, which was slow, difficult and unconventional but gave brilliant luminosity to their colours. Rossetti tended to use colour symbolically but Hunt based his colours on an uncompromisingly fresh study of the natural world. Hunt also painted the accessories with a myopic attention to the smallest detail not simply for the sake of realism but because, like all the Pre-Raphaelites, he elaborated the subject of the picture, as Van Eyck did, in the form of hidden symbols.

Differences of temperament and an inevitable weakening of their youthful enthusiasm for conspiracy led to the breakup of the Brotherhood in

8

the early 50s. The Pre-Raphaelite labour of the hand and eye became too troublesome for Rossetti who began to specialise in visionary scenes, inspired by poetic sources, painted in gouache. Millais, too, following his marriage to Ruskin's ex-wife in 1855, gave up the time-consuming techniques of the Brotherhood for the vilified but conveniently rapid manner of Reynolds and Velasquez. Stephens became a writer. Collinson, after a spell as a novice in a Roman Catholic monastery, became a conventional genre painter. Of the founders of the original Brotherhood, only Hunt remained true to his principles of earnest hard-work and high-minded themes while Rossetti's decorative, poetic work offered an exciting and less laborious alternative to a younger generation.

As will become clear from this book the Pre-Raphaelites were closely connected with Oxford. The religious sentiment and symbolism of their first works owed much to the High Church Revival – the Oxford Movement – and in all its phases Pre-Raphaelite art owed something to John Ruskin who was an undergraduate at Christ Church and returned later in his life to the University as Slade Professor. Some of the Pre-Raphaelites' earliest and most important patrons lived in Oxford – above all Thomas Combe whose collection of paintings is now in the Ashmolean Museum. It was in the Oxford Union that their most important attempt at mural painting was made. Burne-Jones and Morris discovered Rossetti's art when they were undergraduates in Exeter College and the Aesthetic movement into which one strand of Pre-Raphaeliteism developed, originated in Oxford.

Ford Madox Brown 1821–1893

1   *The Seeds and Fruits of English Poetry*
Oil on canvas, 36 × 46 cm
Inscribed: FORD MADOX BROWN DEST IN ROMA. 1845. COLORAVIT
IN HAMPSTEAD. 1853.

Seeds and Fruits was planned in London and composed in Rome in 1845. 'During my sojourn', Brown recalled, 'Italian art had made a deep and, as it proved, lasting impression on me, for I never afterwards returned to the sombre, Rembrandtesque style I had formerly worked in'. The influence of the Italian artists before Raphael is obvious in the triptych-like format, in the gothic arches, in the six poets arranged like saints on a gold ground in the wings of a medieval altar piece and in the bright colour. However, in 1851, when Brown finished the large picture, for which this is a study, he omitted all the gothic detail and, later, justified the bright colour as a novel attempt to introduce effects of bright sunlight into painting. Brown, by the early 50s, had succumbed to the Pre-Raphaelite ideal of 'truth to nature' but not before he had given his disciple, Rossetti, a lasting taste for the art of the 'Early Christians'.

The centre panel shows Chaucer reading at the court of Edward III with his patron, the Black Prince, on his left. In the wings appear the 'fruits' of English poetry: Milton, Spenser and Shakespeare on the left; Byron, Pope and Burns on the right; Goldsmith and Thomson in the roundels; and the names of Campbell, Moore, Shelley, Keats, Chatterton, Kirke White, Coleridge and Wordsworth are written on the cartouches held by the standing children in the base.

10

John Everett Millais 1829–1896

2   *Portrait of Ford Madox Brown*
Water-colours over pencil, 11.4 cm
Inscribed: JEM 1853.

Although older than the other Pre-Raphaelites and never
formally admitted to the Brotherhood, Brown was an
important member of the circle.

John Everett Millais

The Apple Gatherers

12

13

Ford Madox Brown

3   *The Pretty Baa-lambs*
Oil on panel, 20 × 26 cm
Inscribed: F Madox Brown. 52

The Pre-Raphaelite passion for accurate observation brought artists into the open air with their paint and canvas. Brown began the original *Baa-lambs*, of which this is a variant, in 1851, posing his lay figure in hot sunlight at his home in Stockwell. His wife, Emma, and their daughter, Catherine, posed for the main group. The sheep, brought over each day from Clapham Common, ate all the flowers in his garden and the hot sunshine gave the artist a fever. Brown was not the first, nor the last, Pre-Raphaelite to discover the trials of working out of doors. The rich, sun-drenched effect was, as Brown insisted, the main subject of this picture but, if so, it is not obvious why the figures are dressed in eighteenth century costume. The Ashmolean picture, painted in the studio of Thomas Seddon in 1852, is a small replica of the original, now in Birmingham. The background probably shows the appearance of the Birmingham picture before the landscape in it was extensively repainted in 1859 by the artist.

14

Arthur Hughes 1832–1915

4   *The Eve of St. Agnes* (centre panel)
Oil on board, 27 × 31 cm

This picture is a study for a larger triptych (now in the Tate Gallery) which Hughes exhibited in 1856. The study originally belonged to the sculptor, Alexander Munro, with whom Hughes shared a studio in the mid 1850s. The combined types of lighting in the episodes which Hughes selected from Keats's poem, recall Hunt's preoccupation with similar effects. The division of the composition into three panels, in the manner of a medieval alterpiece, was, no doubt, inspired by Brown (see fig. 1) and Rossetti. Hunt, too, certainly inspired the right hand panel, the escape of Porphyro and Madeline from the castle, which Hunt had painted in 1848. But Hughes depicted Keats's *Eve of St. Agnes* with a sensitivity to the verse that was alien to Hunt (who was the least poetic of the group) and to Rossetti who imposed his personal vision on everything he painted. Like Millais, he had a marvellous talent for illustration and did his most interesting work, after the 1850s, for publishers.

Arthur Hughes

5   *Home from Sea*
Oil on panel, 50 × 65 cm
Inscribed: ARTHUR HUGHES 1862

Hughes, who met Brown, Hunt and Rossetti for the first time in 1850, was an early convert to the art of the Brotherhood. Although less ambitious in his choice of subjects than his friends, he knew how to invest the fresh, light-filled detail of the English landscape with the poignancy of ordinary life. The background of *Home from Sea* was painted in the graveyard of Chingford Church, Essex, in 1856. He exhibited it in 1857 as *A Mother's Grave*. The appearance of the picture, at this stage, is known from a study, by Hughes, in the Ashmolean [see below]. Later, perhaps in response to critics who did not like the way the boy was painted, he added the figure of his sister, which is modelled on his wife, and exhibited this revised version at the Royal Academy in 1863 with the present title. In keeping with the Pre-Raphaelite practise, the detail is not gratuitous but is used to reinforce the pathos of the subject. Ephemeral things – the spider's web, wet with dew, the dog roses, the dandelion seed – all draw attention to the theme of transience while the boy's loss is retold, allusively, in the detail of the sheep separated from its lamb by the barrier of the tomb.

18

John William Inchbold 1830–1888

6   *A Study in March*
Oil on canvas 53 × 35 cm
Inscribed: JWI

Exhibited in 1855 with lines from the first book of
Wordsworth's *The Excursion:*
       'When the primrose flower
       Peeped forth to give an earnest of the Spring.'

It has been pointed out that the concentration on
the detail of the foreground distinguishes Pre-Raphaelite
landscapes from the older, pastoral tradition in which the
foreground is generally sacrificed to the middle distance.
Despite the danger of spoiling the unity of the composition
by working piece-meal on the details, Inchbold achieves
an astonishing balance of detail and atmosphere, unified
through the delicacy of touch and the natural luminosity
of the colour, thinly laid onto a white ground in the
manner of the Brotherhood. Ruskin, whose influence is
evident throughout the composition, described the effect
as 'exceedingly beautiful'.

John William Inchbold

7   *The Cuillin Ridge, Skye*
Oil on canvas 51 × 69 cm
Inscribed: J.W. INCHBOLD

This undated landscape has been identified as *The Burn,
November – The Cucullen Hills* which Inchbold exhibited
at the Royal Academy in 1856. As in *A Study in March,* the
real subject, the burn of the title, is concentrated in the
foreground. Also, as in the earlier picture, the landscape
depicts the light and weather of a particular month, in
this case, the chill, sharp light of a November day in
North-West Scotland when the sun hardly rises above
the horizon. Ruskin, who praised the 'exquisite painting
of withered heather and rock' in *The Cuillin Ridge,*
commissioned four drawings from the artist and spent
two weeks with him in Switzerland in 1858. 'It was'
recalled Ruskin, 'a delicate and difficult matter to make
him gradually find out his own faults . . . and took me a
fortnight of innuendoes. At last I think I succeeded in
making him entirely uncomfortable and ashamed of
himself and then left him.' It is not obvious that Inchbold
was improved by this advice. It is more probable that the
'fortnight of innuendoes' and Ruskin's subsequent in-
difference to his work profoundly discouraged Inchbold,
who had an awkward and retiring character and who
never fulfilled the promise of his early paintings.

Thomas Combe

The link between Oxford and the Pre-Raphaelites
was made first by Millais who arrived in 1846 to
visit his half brother. At Oxford, Millais met his first
patron, the art dealer and framer, James Wyatt, who
provided him with studio space in the High Street in
1849 and commissioned portraits of himself and his
family. Millais was not yet a Pre-Raphaelite when he
met Wyatt and the most important picture bought by
Wyatt from Millais, his *Cymon and Iphigenia,* was
painted in the manner of older, academic artists. But
Wyatt's support gave Oxford an important place in
Millais's earliest Pre-Raphaelite compositions. *Christ
in the Carpenter's Shop* was, according to Hunt,
inspired by a sermon heard in Oxford and a window
in *Mariana* is based on one in Merton College. But it
was the landscape of Oxford, the woodlands of
Botley and Shotover, which were of real use to the
artist who, like Hunt and his friends, often painted
the background of pictures in the open air. Oxford
also provided the Pre-Raphaelites with their first
major patron, Thomas Combe, who made friends
with Millais and with his disciple, Charles Allston
Collins, in 1850, while the two young artists were
painting at Botley. Combe, who made his fortune
as printer to the University from 1838 to 1872, spent
part of it in building a school and churches for the
families of his employees. He supported 'The Oxford
Movement', a reforming group within the Church of
England which bitterly divided English society in the
mid century by attempting to reverse the effects of
the Reformation on the liturgy. The hint of Catholic
or 'High Church' bias which disturbed some critics
in the works of the Pre-Raphaelites, could only have
attracted Combe. In the first instance, however, the

Combes were probably not drawn to the philosphy of the Brotherhood as much as they were drawn to Millais's youthful talent and aimiable character. Millais, then, took the initiative, teaching his wealthy friends to appreciate the merits of the Pre-Raphaelites at a time when their reputation was in the balance. By the end of September, 1850, Collins and Millais had both moved into Combe's house in Walton Street where Millais painted Combe's portrait and Collins finished the garden in the background of his *Convent Thoughts*.

John Everett Millais

8   *Portrait of Thomas Combe*
Oil on panel, 33 × 27 cm
Inscribed with the artist's monogram and dated: 1850.

Millais and Collins met Combe while they were painting
out of doors at Botley in 1850. Mrs Combe, an ex-pupil of
the watercolourist, David Cox, presided over a good
humoured Salon in her house at the University Press in
Walton Street where this portrait, and a companion
portrait, by Collins, of Martha Combe's uncle, William
Bennett, were painted. According to a label in Combe's
handwriting on the back, Millais painted this portrait in
four sittings of two hours each. The coat-of-arms is that
granted in 1584 to John Combe of Stratford, a friend of
Shakespeare. Combe denied any connection with his
namesake when Hunt asked him about this. But he was
apparently interested in heraldry and decorated the
drawing room where his Pre-Raphaelite collection was
displayed with a frieze of fifty-nine metal shields representing the arms of the knights who fell at the battle of
Caerlaverock.

Charles Allston Collins

*The artist and J.E. Millais
with Thomas and Martha
Combe and William Bennett*

William Holman Hunt 1827–1910

9   *A Converted British Family Sheltering a Christian Missionary from the persecution of the Druids*
Oil on canvas, 111 × 141 cm
Inscribed: W. HOLMAN HUNT/1850

Critics savaged the work of the Brotherhood at the Royal Academy exhibition of 1850 as ugly, incompetent and blasphemous. This was a severe blow to the hopes of the young artists. Fortunately Millais had sold his *Christ in the Carpenter's Shop* to a dealer before the exhibition opened, but Hunt's *Converted British Family* returned, unsold, to his studio. The picture started life in 1849 as an academic set piece on the theme of Mercy but evolved as Hunt's first major exercise in Pre-Raphaelite painting, illustrating, in symbolic form, the humanizing effects of Christianity. The priest, a first century missionary from Israel, shelters in the house of the converts while a fellow missionary in the background is driven from the precint of the Druid's shrine. Hunt took trouble to make the scene as historical and plausible as he could. At the same time, he invested the composition with complex allusions to the Christian mission. The priest, in the foreground, is presented as the type of the persecuted Christ. The central group recalls the *Pietà*, the traditional representation of the Virgin grieving over Christ. The thorns and sponge refer to Christ's passion; the vine, too, is an attribute of Christ. This theme is reinforced by the Biblical texts inscribed by Hunt on the frame which refer to salvation through suffering and to the quality of mercy. This elaborate symbolism, with more than a hint of the High Church, may explain why Millais told Mrs Combe's uncle, William Bennett, that it would make an appropriate present for his niece's husband. Combe evidently approved of the idea. It was his first important Pre-Raphaelite acquisition. In a long account of the work, sent to Combe in 1851, Hunt explained that the corn and the cabbages on the right were intended as an allusion to the civilising effects of Christianity while the nets, hanging over the water, refer to the mission of the apostles as 'fishers of men'.

John Everett Millais

10   *The Return of the Dove to the Ark*
Oil on canvas, 88 × 55 cm
Inscribed: J Millais 1851

In 1880, Millais began work on an ambitious picture on
the theme of the Deluge. His plans for this are known
from an expressive drawing in the British Museum and
from his letters to Combe in which Millais told his patron
that it would compare favourably with a sermon. Millais
abandoned this idea and turned instead to a scene inside
the Ark in which he intended to include 'several birds and
animals, one of which now forms the prey to the other'.
But sermonising was not Millais's speciality and he finally
adopted the present, less rhetorical solution in which the
background, by Pre-Raphaelite standards, is untypically
dark. But the detail that remains, the drapery and straw,
are painted with astonishing virtuosity. Ruskin, who saw
it at the Royal Academy exhibition in 1851, had hoped to
buy it, but it had already been sold to Combe, in March,
before the opening of his exhibition. Combe hung it on a
white wall in his drawing room, on one side of Hunt's
Converted British Family with Collins's *Convent Thoughts*
on the other side.

Charles Allston Collins 1828–1873

11   *Convent Thoughts*
Oil on canvas, 84 × 59 cm
Inscribed with the artist's monogram and dated: 51.

Charles Allston Collins, son of the academician, William
Collins (and brother of Wilkie Collins, the novelist) was a
conventionally academic painter before his friendship
with Millais in 1850 led him to change his manner. The
background of *Convent Thoughts* was begun in Botley in
1850 when Collins was visiting Oxford with Millais.
According to a note by Thomas Combe on the back, the
flowers were painted in Combe's garden in Walton
Street. The novice was added later, in London using a
costume which Hunt had previously used in *Claudio and
Isabella*. The sleeves, however, covered the essential
missal which the novice holds. Collins admitted that he
was tempted to cut the sleeves short: 'It is awkward' he
wrote 'in as much as part of the story depends on the
hand and the book held in it'. The book, indeed, provides
the key to the symbolism. The novice's index finger marks
a page illustrating the *Annunciation*, the moment when
the angel tells the Virgin that she has been set aside for
special grace. She is surrounded by many different
species of lily flowers, the Virgin's attribute, which also
flank the picture on the frame, designed by Millais and
inscribed 'Sicut Lilium', the opening words of a text from
the Song of Solomon, conventionally thought to prefigure
the Virgin of the New Testament: 'As the lily among
Thorns, so is my love among the daughters'. The flower
she holds, however, is a Passion Flower, symbol of the
Crucifixion, to which her thoughts have turned. We
know this as the missal is open at a picture of the
Crucifixion.
  Convent Thoughts was exhibited at the Royal
Academy of 1851 along with Millais's *Return of the Dove*
and Hunt's *Valentine Rescuing Sylvia*. All three were
severely attacked by the critics. Millais, again, persuaded
Combe to come to the rescue by buying *Convent
Thoughts* while Coventry Patmore wrote to Ruskin
asking him to write something in the press about the
painters who were attempting to paint nature according
to his own precepts. Ruskin complied with a famous
letter to *The Times* (13 May 1851) in which he warmly
defended Collins's botany while glossing over his evident
sympathy for Roman Catholicism.

32

William Holman Hunt

12   *The Light of the World*
Oil on canvas, 125 × 59 cm
Inscribed: WHH 1853; and (behind frame): Non me
Praetermisso Domine.
Reproduced by kind permission of the Warden and
Fellows of Keble College, Oxford

The subject was inspired by a text from Revelation:
'Behold, I stand at the door, and knock: if any man hear
my voice, and open the door, I will come in to him, and
will sup with him, and he with me.' Hunt probably knew a
print after a picture on the theme by Philipp Viet,
composed in the Early Christian manner of the Nazarenes.
Hunt's picture, however, was painted according to
different, Pre-Raphaelite principles of painstakingly
detailed observation. He set the scene in the hour before
the dawn to indicate the coming of the Saviour in keeping
with the text: 'The night is far spent, the day is at hand'.
(Romans, 13:12). This indicated the lantern and, also, the
picture's final title. The winter setting suggests man's lack
of grace and the promise of Salvation. Hunt painted the
landscape in the orchard of Worcester Park Farm in
Surrey, in November and December, 1851, working from
9 pm to 5 am, protected from the cold by a straw hut; he
completed the figure in his studio in 1853, using a white
robe made from a tablecloth and a brass lamp, made to
his design, which gave the artist (and his model) a great
deal of trouble by smoking, overheating and going out.
Much of the symbolism is obvious: the door of the hut has
no handle on the outside so that it can only be opened by
the soul within; the weeds indicate that the door had not
been opened for a long time; the apples on the ground
recall the Fall of Man; other less evident references were
explained by Hunt and his friends: the bat, above the
door, represents ignorance (because it loves the dark);
Christ's clasp represents the tribes of Israel (in the
rectangle) joined to paganism (in the circle) by the five
wounds of Christ; the seven-sided lantern indicates the
seven Churches mentioned in Revelation. Hunt, who met
Combe for the first time while painting the *Light of the
World,* told him that he had worked on it throughout
'with the hope that it might find its resting place in
Oxford'. Combe bought it for four hundred guineas in
1853. After his death, Mrs Combe gave it to Keble College
(built in 1868–82 in memory of John Keble, a pioneer of
the High Church Movement) where it was installed in a
side chapel, specially built for it, with a bequest from Mrs
Combe, in 1895.

William Holman Hunt

13   *The Afterglow in Egypt*
Oil on canvas, 82 × 37 cm
Inscribed with the artist's monogram

On 13 January 1854, financed by the sale of his
paintings, Hunt left England to travel for two years in the
Near East hoping to rediscover the landscape of the Bible
in Egypt and Palestine. The heat and dust of Egypt and
the Holy Land proved even worse than the cold of
England to the determined Pre-Raphaelite. Writing from
Egypt in 1854, Hunt told Combe that he had begun 'a
study of an Egyptian girl the size of life which however
what with the difficulty of getting the model day by day
and the horrible trials of wind and dust even in the best
places I can find for painting in – is in danger of being
abandoned – at least for the present.' He returned to the
unfinished work (now in Southampton Art Gallery) in
1861, adding the lower half and painting the Ashmolean
version at the same time. Where the model in the
Southampton picture carries a sheaf of wheat, she now
carries a cage of pigeons; the calf and cow are additions;
and the position of her feet has changed, making her less
statuesque. There is probably no special symbolism in
the figure although Hunt admitted that he had posed the
original model with ancient Egyptian statuary in mind.
This debt to Egyptian art is more evident in the
Southampton picture than it is in the Ashmolean version
where Hunt, displeased, perhaps, with the rigidity of the
original, has introduced a not altogether successful effect
of swaying movement. Combe bought this second
version after Hunt had, unsuccessfully, offered to sell it
for three hundred guineas to another patron, Thomas
Plint, in 1861.

William Holman Hunt

14   *The School-Girl's Hymn*
Oil on panel, 35 × 25 cm
Inscribed: 18 WHH 59

The origin of this picture is given in a note, pasted to the back of the panel, by Combe: 'This represents a girl going to school on a smiling summer Sunday morning, singing her hymn as she walks along. In the summer of 1858, Hunt went to see his friend who was staying at a farmhouse in the neighbourhood of Hastings, he then began this picture which was not finished till 1859. It is a portrait of Miriam Wilkinson, a labourer's daughter – in the spring of 1859 she came up to Kensington that he might finish it.' The picture was finished in October and sent to an exhibition, organised by Ernest Gambart, in November. Combe bought it before the opening. In a letter to Gambart and in another to the keeper of the University Galleries in Oxford, Hunt connected the subject with four lines from Coventry Patmore's *Tamerton Church Tower.*
'It was an almshouse scholar trim
who on her happy way,
Sang to herself the morrow's hymn,
For this was Saturday.'

She sings from a book inscribed PSALMS AND HYMNS. But Patmore was probably an afterthought. Hunt, who retouched the picture in 1860 for Combe, referred to it always as a 'pot-boiler', a picture to earn money while the more serious and time-consuming business of his bigger pictures was in hand.

William Holman Hunt

15   *London Bridge on the Night of the Marriage of the*
      Prince and Princess of Wales
Oil on canvas, 65 × 98 cm
Inscribed with artist's monogram and dated 1863–6

Hunt was present in the crowd on London Bridge on the
night of 10 March 1863, celebrating the marriage of
Princess Alexandra of Denmark to the future Edward VII.
'The display' Hunt recalled 'made many buildings, by
daylight dingy with city smoke, fairy-like and gorgeous.
Temple Bar was enlivened by hangings of gold and silver
tissue and London Bridge was hung with masts, crimson
banners surmounting the Danish insignia of the Elephant;
tripod braziers and groups of statuary made up the show
of welcome to the Princess on the spot full of memories of
Danish exploits of ancient times, and the whole was
illuminated by an effulgence of light. Being fascinated by
the picturesque scene, I made sketches of it in my note-
book, and the next day I recorded them with colour on a
canvas. When I had completed this, the Hogarthian
humour that I had seen tempted me to introduce the
crowd; but to do this at all adequately, grew to be a heavy
undertaking'. The picture was not ready for exhibition
until 16 May 1864 and was retouched in 1866. The
'Hogarthian' element (which surprised the critics) reflects
Hunt's interest in the 'stalwart founder of Modern
English Art' as he described Hogarth. This was not Pre-
Raphaelitism as Rossetti understood it, but Hogarth's art
of moral commentary was congenial to Hunt and his
friends who named a short lived club for Pre-Raphaelite
artists and their friends after him. However, as Hunt's
account of the scene shows, he was initially attracted to
the different effects of natural and artifical lighting
combined here, as they are combined in *The Light of the
World*, in a single composition. Hunt included portraits
of the Combes, along with portraits of other friends in the
lower left. This probably encouraged Mrs Combe to buy
the picture from the artist after the death of Thomas
Combe in 1872. The frame was designed by Hunt with
appropriate emblems for a wedding, combined with the
royal arms of Denmark and of England.

40

The Union murals

In 1855, Rossetti finally arrived in Oxford, following
Elizabeth Siddal who had gone there on Ruskin's
advice to consult Dr. Henry Acland on the subject
of her ill-health. Both were warmly received within
the University but not by the Combes who clearly
preferred the sober minded Hunt to his Bohemian
friends. Combe bought Rossetti's *Dante drawing an
Angel* in 1855, but this was the only work by Rossetti
in his collection. Ruskin, however, seeing *Beatrice
meeting Dante at a Wedding Feast* at an exhibition
in 1852, was converted by his seductive colour and
became an important ally. An attempt was made
to involve Rossetti in decorating the interior of
Benjamin Woodward's University Museum, a project
in which Ruskin and Acland were deeply involved,
but this came to nothing perhaps because the subject
suggested to Rossetti, *Newton gathering pebbles on
the Shore of the Ocean of Truth,* was not his taste.
However, the idea of painting on a wall must have
appealed to Rossetti since he offered, instead, to
decorate the interior of the Debating Room (now
the library) in Woodward's recently completed
Union building, in return for nothing but board and
lodging. Rossetti brought in six followers to help him
to decorate the gallery of the neo-gothic hall with
scenes from the Arthurian legends. Apart from
Rossetti and Arthur Hughes, none of the team (which
included Edward Burne-Jones, William Morris,
J.H. Pollen, Valentine Prinsep and Spencer Stanhope)
had much previous experience of painting and the
mural was abandoned, unfinished, in the Spring
of 1858. The Union employed a local artist, William
Riviere and his son Briton, a future Royal
Academician, to complete the scheme in the

following year. The idea of painting something like an old Italian fresco must have appealed to Rossetti but neither he, nor any of the artists who worked on the murals, had any clear idea of the problems of painting on a wall. They used tempera paint, applied with small brushes directly onto a dry, ill-prepared brick surface and within ten years, the surface had deteriorated. Despite two extensive restorations, the murals are now only a shadow of the colourful originals which were described by Patmore, a colleague of the Brotherhood, as 'sweet, bright and pure as that of the frailest waif of cloud in the sunrise.'

Dante Gabriel Rossetti 1828–1882

16   *Portrait of Elizabeth Siddal*
Pen and brown and black ink with wash, 12 × 11 cm
Inscribed: DGR Feb 6 1855

Elizabeth Siddal was an assistant in a millinery shop in
London when Walter Deverell first employed her as a
model. She met Rossetti in 1850 and became his favourite
model, his mistress and his pupil. As well as drawing in
the manner of Rossetti, she wrote poetry in the style of
Rossetti's sister, Christina. When Rossetti drew this
portrait in 1855, she was a confirmed invalid although the
nature of her illness was never convincingly diagnosed.
Her Oxford physician, Dr Acland suspected it was self-
induced. She married Rossetti in 1860 and died two years
later from an overdose of laudanum. Rossetti's portrait
recalls Georgiana Burne-Jones's description of her at
this time:
'She wore her hair very loosely fastened up, so that it fell
in soft heavy wings. Her complexion looked as if a rose
tint lay beneath the dark skin, producing a most soft and
delicate pink for the darkest flesh tones. Her eyes were of
a kind of golden brown . . . and wonderfully luminous: in
all Gabriel's drawings of her and in the type she created
in his mind this is to be seen. Her eyelids were deep, but
without any langour or drowsiness, and had the peculiarity
of seeming scarcely to veil the light in her eyes when
looking down'.

45

Dante Gabriel Rossetti

17   *Dante drawing an Angel on the First Anniversary of
the Death of Beatrice*
Water-colour, 42 × 61 cm
Inscribed: DGR/1853.

Influenced by Hunt, Rossetti began work in 1853 on a
subject from modern, urban life but did not finish it,
finding a more congenial and less demanding form of art
in a series of finished water-colours, inspired by medieval
sources, which he painted in the 1850s. Rossetti had
already made two drawings with the same subject as this
large water-colour to illustrate an episode in Dante's *Vita
Nuova*: while drawing an angel on the anniversary of
Beatrice's death, Dante looks round to find 'that some
were standing beside me to whom I should have given
courteous welcome – – – Perceiving whom, I rose for
salutation and said: "Another was with me." 'Among the
visitors, Rossetti included a woman who is not mentioned
in the text but who was intended to represent Dante's
future wife, Gemma Donati, although Rossetti, himself,
was in two minds about this. Elizabeth Siddal modelled
for this figure, proving, at least, that Rossetti was not
then wholly committed to the idea of identifying her with
Beatrice. The accessories illustrate different aspects of
the narrative; the ivy is probably an emblem of memory;
the skull represents death; the hour glass indicates
passing time; the pomegranate is an emblem of Proserpine;
the book recalls Virgil's role in the *Divine Comedy*. Along
with this Pre-Raphaelite detail, there is a tendency to
flatness, particularly noticeable in the frieze of angel
heads, which is common to all Rossetti's water-colours in
this period. Both Combe and Ruskin liked this composition
but Rossetti had already sold it for fifty pounds to Francis
McCracken, an early collector of Pre-Raphaelite art.
Combe bought it at McCracken's sale in 1855.

18   *Beatrice, meeting Dante at a Wedding Feast, denies*
     him her Salutation
Water-colour, 34 × 42 cm

In 1848, Rossetti included this subject in a list of proposed illustrations for his translation of Dante's *Vita Nuova*. He exhibited a water-colour on the same theme in 1852 at the gallery of the dealer, Ernest Gambart, where Ruskin saw it. This was Ruskin's first chance to assess the work of Rossetti. He told Holman Hunt that it was 'a *most glorious* piece of colour. The breadth of blue – green – fragmentary gold is a perfect feast.' Rossetti borrowed his water-colour from its first owner in 1855 to make this second, nearly identical version for a client, but Ruskin, in the interim, bought it for himself. The composition follows the broad outlines of Dante's text which describes how the author was overcome by a faint while watching a marriage procession with a friend. 'Whereupon I remember that I covertly leaned my back into a painting that ran round the walls of that house; and being fearful lest my trembling should be discerned of them, I lifted mine eyes to look on those ladies, and then first perceived among them the excellent Beatrice – – – many of her friends, having perceived my confusion, began to wonder; and together with herself, kept whispering of me and mocking me.' Rossetti combined this passage with an earlier episode in which Beatrice, misunderstanding Dante's behaviour, withholds her salutation. Rossetti also added the little girl offering her flowers to Dante as a foil to the scornful attitude of Beatrice.

Dante Gabriel Rossetti

19   *Sir Lancelot's Vision of the Sanc Grael*
Water-colour and body colour over black chalk,
71 × 107 cm

In 1857, Rossetti chose the theme of Malory's *Morte d'Arthur* to decorate the ten gallery bays of the Union debating hall, promising, optimistically, to paint three of them himself. Of these three – *Sir Galahad receiving the Sanc Grael, Lancelot found in Guenevere's Chamber* and *Sir Lancelot asleep before the Shrine of the Sanc Grael* – only the last, for which this is a preparatory drawing, was more or less finished when Rossetti left Oxford in November. The original is now a ruin but, in the brief period while it was still visible, it was much admired, especially by poetry-minded students at the University. Rossetti, who was an instinctive pattern-maker, made a virtue of the hexafoil windows which awkwardly divide the wall into three areas; on the right, Lancelot lies sleeping; on the left is the shrine of the angels while the vision of Queen Guenevere, holding up the tempting fruit, like Eve, towards the sleeping knight, separates the two, just as, in the narrative, she came between Lancelot and the fulfilment of his quest to find the holy grail.

Morris and Burne-Jones

William Morris and Edward Burne-Jones both came
up to Exeter College in Oxford, in 1853, intending to
take holy orders, but the works of Ruskin and the
sight of Pre-Raphaelite paintings in Wyatt's shop and
in Combe's house converted them to the cause of art.
Like other students at the time, they were especially
impressed by Rossetti whose *Dante drawing an
Angel,* a recent addition to Combe's collection, filled
them with 'wonder and delight'. They shared his
nostalgia for medieval art and poetry which they
imitated more attentively than the Pre-Raphaelites
of 1848 had ever done. When Morris decided to train
as an architect, he turned in 1856 to one of the most
inventive neo-Gothic architects of the time, George
Edmund Street, who had an office in Beaumont
Street. Here Morris met Street's senior clerk, Philip
Webb, the future architect, who designed the
'Red House' at Bexley Heath for Morris following
his marriage to Jane Burden in 1859. Webb also
designed furniture for Morris's rooms, first in 17 Red
Lion Square and then for the Red House, massive
mock-medieval pieces, some of which were
decorated by Rossetti, Morris and Burne-Jones in
a strong, flat, heraldic style.

Burne-Jones, meanwhile, took lessons in
painting from Rossetti, developing Rossetti's
languorous ideal and sense of pattern, firstly in
gouache drawings, then in paintings and above all,
in the designs which he supplied to the firm of Morris,
Meade, Marshall and Faulkener, founded in 1861,
with Rossetti, Burne-Jones and Brown as partners.
This enterprise, which originated in the furniture
commissioned by Morris from his friends for his
own rooms, was based on principles of clear, simple

design and on the revival of craft skills. Despite a serious lack of capital in the early years, the firm was, surprisingly, a commercial success and lastingly influenced attitudes to design in England and elsewhere. For an idealist, Morris had an unusual talent for making money. His poems were immensely popular. The Kelmscott Press, founded in 1890 to improve standards of book production, made England, at the end of the century, the centre of art book publishing. But, perhaps because he had never been short of money, he was not satisfied with material success. His ambition to recreate English society in the image of a pre-industrial ideal – an ambition which runs through the history of the Gothic Revival in the nineteenth century, from Pugin and Ruskin to Morris and his followers – was not to be realised by selling expensive, hand-crafted furniture to rich people, and he turned, as others did, to the politics of socialism to find the elusive solution to the problems of the modern world.

Dante Gabriel Rossetti

20   *Proserpine*
Red and black chalks, 97 × 46 cm
Inscribed: DGR 1871

During the summer of 1857, Burne-Jones and Rossetti
met Jane Burden for the first time at the Oxford theatre.
She became a favourite model in Rossetti's circle and
married William Morris in 1859. Her heavy features and
full, black hair became the Pre-Raphaelite ideal of beauty
from this time on, particularly for Rossetti who became
her lover and who painted her obsessively in his late
works. In about 1868, Rossetti began to use her features
in a series of large portraits drawn in red and black chalk,
to which he added poetic and mythological attributes.
This finished drawing relates closely to a painting which
once belonged to L.S. Lowry although it lacks the ivy
tendril, representing 'clinging memory' and the incense
burner, the 'attribute of a goddess' which appear in the
painting. The light square behind her head represents a
shaft of light from the upper world which Proserpine,
according to the myth, unwittingly forfeited by biting
into the fatal pomegranate. Rossetti bequeathed the
drawing to the sitter. Her daughter, May Morris, bequeathed it in 1939 to the Ashmolean in keeping with her
mother's wish.

Edward Burne-Jones 1833–1898

21   *Cabinet decorated with scenes from 'The Prioress's Tale'*
Oak and deal, painted in oil
Inscribed: EBJ to WM; with texts from Chaucer

According to Jane Burden, this cabinet was given as a wedding present to Morris by Burne-Jones. It was placed, at first, in the principal bedroom of the Red House and followed the Morrises when they moved to London in 1865. Painted presumably, in 1858–9, using Jane Burden as a model, it was Burne-Jones most ambitious painting to date. The folding door on the left is inscribed with the opening verses of Chaucer's *Prioress's Tale* and decorated with different episodes from the poem which decribes how a Christian boy, who had learned to sing the hymn *Alma Redemptoris* at his school, was assassinated by resentful Jews. But the Virgin, by placing a grain upon his tongue, allowed him to continue singing and reveal the crime. The Virgin, placing the grain upon his tongue, appears in the centre of the door. She also appears with angels on the right hand door, over a portrait of Chaucer, holding a stalk of wheat.

It is hard to imagine what inspired Burne-Jones to paint a cabinet with such a disagreeable tale although he did it with an instinctive sense of pattern and a Flemish feeling for the detail and thought well enough of the result to repeat the composition in a later painting.

A series of six, unfinished figures, painted by Morris on the inside of the doors, more appropriately refer to the activities of a dressing room. One of these is a variant of Morris's painting, *Queen Guenevere* of 1858. If the painting on the door is the earlier of the two, this would explain the choice of subject in the finished picture which depicts Jane Burden as Queen Guenevere disrobing in a medieval chamber.

Edward Burne-Jones

22   *An Angel Organist*
Brown and blue washes over pencil, 55 × 58 cm
Inscribed: Lyndhurst 1862, no. 42 Top, F.P.

In 1862–3, Morris's firm designed and supplied the glass
for a large, complex east window for St. Michael's
Church in Lyndhurst, Hampshire. The tall, main lights
are surmounted by a round window, encircled with six
trefoils, all glazed following the designs of Burne-Jones.
This is the full scale working drawing for the glass in the
lowest of the trefoils. There is a similar drawing for an
upper trefoil in the Ashmolean [see below] and there are
other drawings for the window in Birmingham City Art
Gallery, in the Fitzwilliam in Cambridge and in the
William Morris Gallery in Walthamstow.

Edward Burne-Jones

23   *Love Leading Alcestis*
Black chalk and water-colour, 135 × 135 cm

In 1863 Ruskin told his friends that he wished to leave England for ever and settle in his beloved Swiss Alps. Burne-Jones suggested that he should build a house, instead, in the Wye Valley and offered to design a set of needlework hangings, illustrating Chaucer's *Legend of Good Women,* for one of the rooms. 'First will come Chaucer, looking frightened according to the poem and inditing the poem with a thrush on his shoulder – then comes Love a little angry, bringing Alcestis. Chaucer in black, Love in red and white and Alcestis in green.' Alcestis, in Greek mythology, sacrificed her life to save her husband, Admetus. She became the archetype of the loving wife. It is quite possible that Burne-Jones designed the set to console Ruskin who had been abandoned by his first wife in favour of Millais. The scheme did not come to much and nothing now remains except a number of full scale drawings, designed by Burne-Jones as needlework patterns for the girls at Winnington Hall, a school in Cheshire which Ruskin supported. Ruskin, who gave this drawing and one other from the set to the Drawing School in Oxford, used them to illustrate his lecture 'On the present state of Modern Art' given at the British Institution in 1867. The graceful linearity of these drawings reflects Burne-Jones's increasing interest in antique and Renaissance art in the early 60s. Ruskin, who was beginning to tire of Rossetti's gothic manner, suggested that Burne-Jones's interpretation of Alcestis, 'the Greek womanly type of faithfulness and eternity of love' had 'gone further into the meaning of the old Greek myth and . . . given the spirit of the love that lives beyond the grave.'

Edward Burne-Jones

24   *St Catherine with two angels and related scenes*
Stained glass
Christ Church Cathedral
© Paul Woodmansterne Publications Ltd

Burne-Jones drew the working models – the 'cartoons' –
for the fourth and last of his windows in the cathedral at
Oxford, in 1878. The window was installed in memory of
Edith Liddell, daughter of Dean Liddell and sister of Alice
Liddell, the original of Lewis Carroll's *Alice in Wonderland*,
in the east window of the south choir aisle, directly across
from the *St. Cecilia* window, installed to Burne-Jones's
design three years earlier. The earliest of his windows in
the cathedral, the *St. Frideswide* window, was designed
in 1859 for the firm of Powell and Son of Whitefriars, one
of a number of important commissions for stained glass
given to Burne-Jones by Powell before 1861 when he
began to work exclusively for Morris. By contrast with
the simple lines, clear forms and bright but restricted
colour of the later windows, the earliest window is richly
subdivided into a mosaic of little details more in keeping
with the medieval tradition of stained glass than his later,
more Italianate designs.

Edward Burne-Jones

St. Frideswide
A study for the figure of
the saint in the upper left
of the St. Frideswide
window in Oxford
cathedral

Edward Burne-Jones

25   *The Star of Bethlehem*
High-warp wool tapestry, 264 × 396 cm
Reproduced by kind permission of the Rector and
Fellows of Exeter College, Oxford

In the late 1880s, Burne-Jones, who had been solely
responsible for the figure work in the firm of Morris and
Co. since 1861, began to design tapestries for Morris.
This was a new development for Morris who added
weaving to the manufacture of stained glass, carpets,
embroidery, tiles, furniture, printed cottons and wallpapers which his workshops produced in increasing
quantities after the firm moved to Merton Abbey, near
London, in 1881. Morris, who abominated the French
habit of reproducing oil paintings in the alien medium of
wool, taught himself the art of weaving and passed the
skill on to his own craftsmen. The *Star of Bethlehem*,
designed in 1887 for the Chapel of Exeter College where
Burne-Jones and Morris had met as undergraduates,
was the firm's first, large-scale attempt at making
tapestry. The pattern of figures, moving up and down the
surface of the tapestry against a rich, flattened background of flowers and trees, recalls the decorative
paintings of Filippo Lippi and his contemporaries in the
early Florentine Renaissance, although there is no direct
source for the composition.

Edward Burne-Jones

26   *Danae and the brazen Tower*
Oil on panel, 38 × 19 cm
Inscribed: E.B.J.

Warned by an oracle that his daughter's son would one
day kill him, Acrisius, King of Argos, imprisoned his
daughter, Danae, in a tower of brass. In due course,
however, she bore a son to Jove who slew his grand-
father as the oracle had predicted. In Burne-Jones's
painting, Danae anxiously watches the workmen enclosing
the tower in curved plates of brass. Like many of Burne-
Jones's Greek subjects, the story was probably not taken
directly from an antique text but from a later source, in
this case, from Morris's *Earthly Paradise* which also
inspired Burne-Jones's series on the theme of Perseus
(Staatsgalerie, Stuttgart), the Pygmalion set (Birmingham
City Museum) and the story of Cupid and Psyche
(Ashmolean).

Edward Burne-Jones

*Psyche gazing at the
sleeping Cupid*
One of forty-seven
illustrations for the tale of
Cupid and
Psyche in Morris's *The
Earthly Paradise*

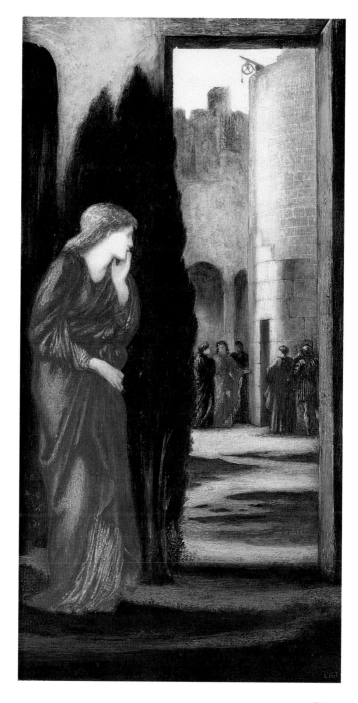

Edward Burne-Jones

27   *Copy of Malory's 'Morte d'Arthur'* with decorated covers, half bound in white pigskin, mahogany boards painted in oil, and silver bosses and clasps, 36 × 26 cm

Malory's *Morte d'Arthur* was a favourite source of subjects for Rossetti and his followers. It provided the inspiration for the Union murals and it gave Morris the theme for his only surviving finished oil painting and the title of his first published book of poetry *The Defense of Guenevere* (1858). Burne-Jones, too, took subjects from Malory for a number of his paintings. This edition, printed by Ballantyne and Hanson after Caxton's edition of 1485 and bound at the Doves Bindery in 1896, came from Burne-Jones's own library in The Grange at Fulham. The front cover has a picture of the round table; the back cover illustrates a knight searching for the holy grail.

Pre-Raphaelites and aesthetes

Millais's links with Oxford and the Combes faded as his London ties increased. Rossetti, too, seems to have lost his taste for Oxford. But Hunt continued to sell his work to the Combes and to visit them in Walton Street. In 1895, he advised the keeper of the University Galleries about the best method for displaying the Pre-Raphaelite collection, bequeathed by Mrs Combe in 1893, and was consulted, again, in 1905, when the collection was rehung against a Morris paper. Ruskin had already given many of his own Pre-Raphaelite drawings to the Art School set up in the University Galleries, largely at the instigation of Dr Acland. These drawings, which were intended to instruct the students in the principles of good taste and right thinking, included an important group by Rossetti as well as forty-seven drawings by Burne-Jones to illustrate a proposed edition of *The Earthly Paradise*. Outside the museum, Burne-Jones's work as a designer can also be seen in the chapel windows at St Edmund Hall and Manchester College and in the cathedral and in the Morris tapestries in Exeter College and Rhodes House.

Perhaps because his work was so accessible or because his art had a languorous charm which appealed to undergraduates and gifted amateurs, it was Burne-Jones, not Hunt who marked the direction which art took in the *fin-de-siècle*. The Middle Ages were not as fashionable then, as they had been, but, in this respect, Burne-Jones had taken the initiative by turning to neo-pagan themes in the early 1860s and by depicting them with the graceful contours which he admired in fifteenth century Renaissance prints and drawings. *The Earthly Paradise* inspired writers of the generation of

Swinburne and Walter Pater whose ideal of beauty, part Greek and part Renaissance, was influenced by the principles of Ruskin. This was also the ideal of artists and designers like Charles Ricketts and Walter Crane who followed Morris in trying to reconcile art and craft at the end of the century. Although many of the younger generation, the aesthetes, who followed Pater into a cult of pure art, tended to reject the earnestness of the Pre-Raphaelites and although the neo-Renaissance taste which they cultivated had other sources apart from Morris and his circle, the cult of design, which affected all aspects of public life in late Victorian England, would not have existed and would not have taken the form it did without the example of the Pre-Raphaelites.

Edward Burne-Jones

28   *Head of a Woman*
Gold paint on purple, prepared ground, 32 × 21 cm

In his later years, Burne-Jones often drew on coloured grounds in imitation of the metal point drawings of the Early Renaissance. Burne-Jones gave this drawing, and a number from the same period, to his close friend, Helen Mary Gaskill, who bequeathed it to the Ashmolean in 1939.

Aubrey Beardsley
1872–1898

A Faun
Designed as a vignette for
an edition of Malory's
Morte d'Arthur

Walter Crane 1845–1915

29   *Shelley's Tomb in the Protestant Cemetery in Rome*
Body colours, 24 × 34 cm
Inscribed: ROMA/1873; and signed in monogram

Crane painted this view of the Protestant cemetery in Rome during his honeymoon in Italy in 1872–3. Like a number of other views which date from this visit, the *Protestant Cemetery* is painted with a Ruskinian eye for detail. Crane, however, had recently met Morris and Burne-Jones for the first time and his art had already begun to move towards the stylised effects of his more familar book illustration and designs for wallpapers, textiles and ceramics. Like William Bell Scott's views of the tombs of Keats and Shelley, also in the Ashmolean, Crane's work acknowledges the cult of these Romantic poets which was not confined to the Pre-Raphaelites but which they appropriated.

John Everett Millais

The Eve of St Agnes
An illustration for
Moxon's edition of the
poems of Tennyson

75

Frederic Sandys 1832–1904

30   *Gentle Spring*
Oil on canvas, 121 × 64 cm

Sandys, a painter and illustrator from Norwich, became a member of Rossetti's circle in 1857. He shared Rossetti's rooms at 16 Cheyne Walk for most of 1866 before quarrelling and parting company with his master. The background of *Gentle Spring* was painted in the garden of the writer, George Meredith, when his friendship with Rossetti was still close. Sandys exhibited it at the Academy exhibition of 1865 with a sonnet by Algernon Swinburne who had joined Rossetti's circle at the same time as Sandys:

'O Virgin Mother! of gentle days and nights
Spring of fresh buds and Spring of soft delights,
Come, with lips kissed of many an amorous hour
Come, with hands heavy from the fervent flower
The fleet first flower that feels the wind and sighs
The tenderer leaf that draws the sun and dies!'

The figure probably represents Proserpine whose return from the Underworld, in Greek mythology, accompanies the return of Spring. Swinburne's poem was inspired by the painting but the poet did not respond to a darker element in Sandys picture indicated by the shadow of winter, draining from the landscape, the poppies, emblems of sleep and death, and the general sense of transience which pervades the details. The landscape is painted with a Pre-Raphaelite truthfulness, but the figure is inspired by Greek or Roman statuary.

Charles de Sousy Ricketts 1866–1931

31   *Pendant*
Gold and enamel, set with semi-precious stones and
linked to three suspended, baroque pearls, 5 cm (diam)
Inscribed: CR

Like Walter Crane, Charles Ricketts was typical of the
artist-craftsman in the generation after Morris who
combined several talents in painting, illustration and
design. Most of his jewellery was made between 1900 and
1908 for specific clients. The Ashmolean pendant was
designed by Ricketts in 1900 for Mrs Llewellyn Hacon,
wife of Rickett's partner in The Vale Press, and made by
Carlo and Arthur Giuliano. It carries her portrait in a
gold medallion, gem-set and enamelled in the manner of
the sixteenth century jewels which Ricketts admired.

Charles Fairfax Murray
1849–1919

*Half-length study of a
woman with a stringed
instrument*

Although there are no footnotes in this book, the text depends heavily on the work of others. Those who wish to know more should consult the following: Allen Staley *The Pre-Raphaelite Landscape* (Oxford 1973), John Christian *The Pre-Raphaelites in Oxford* (Oxford 1974), *The Pre-Raphaelites* (Tate Gallery, 7 March – 28 May 1984), *The Pre-Raphaelites in Oxford* (Tokyo, Shiga, Osaka 1987). I have also received help from Miss Noelle Brown, Mr Michael Maclagan, Dr. Nicholas Penny, Miss J.E. Robinson, Commander S.H. Stone, Miss Lucy Whitaker and Mr Paul Woodmansterne for which I am most grateful. All works of art illustrated are in the Ashmolean Museum unless otherwise stated.